A Whirlwind Dream

By Anna Tempero

Copyright 7 April 2021 Anna Tempero

Instagram: _altwrites
Twitter: Anna_Tempero
Tumblr: alisaslife
Email: anna.tempero@outlook.com

Cover art designed by Lilah Bowers
Instagram: artbylilah

Printed by Printabooks.

Edited by Diana Brett
Email: diana.brett@xtra.co.nz
Instagram: Diana_Brett

IBSN: 978-0-473-57055-2

*For my loyal private instagram followers;
you let me be me from the beginning.*

Prologue

A whirlwind dream, that's how I would describe my life. The following odes provide a look into what dreams and nightmares look like to me. They include broken boys, betrayal, pain, friendship, peace and passion. My dream for this book is to show its readers that it's ok to feel however you feel. Your surroundings also don't have to affect or change how you feel. Often, on the outside, my life would look like a dream, but in my mind I'd be fighting a nightmare.

I hope that my words will have an impact on your life in some way, even if just one of my poems ignites some emotion inside of you. The book is divided into three chapters: nightmares, dreams and our reality. I set it out this way because the dreams and nightmares are all certain experiences I went through, whereas each of the notes in 'our reality' can be applied to anyone. I hope you will find comfort or peace in at least one of the affirmations you read.

The concept of my dreams entails the good times but also the times where I tried to rewrite my realities. Dreams don't always come true, and sometimes the action of dreaming in place of understanding constitutes unhealthy thought habits. Sometimes it was the action of ignoring red flags or simply choosing only to see the good in a terrible situation. I hope this compilation will act as a reminder that life is a journey, and healing is never linear.

A couple of years ago I never would have imagined myself allowing anyone access to this side of my mind, but I am learning that vulnerability and authenticity is so important in today's world. I hope you understand that these words have come from some of my most painful places but also some of my best. Please note that I still love and care for the people within these odes.

Much of my writing has come from a negative place, and I think that stems from an idea that my painful feelings aren't valid because of my natural positivity, especially when I always hope for a better day. Writing out my feelings felt like the only way to express them on some days. Releasing this book allows my story to be heard, while creating a space for me to find deeper healing and personal growth.

Contents

Nightmares 11

Dreams 95

Our Reality 143

NIGHTMARES

NIGHTMARES

A Whirlwind Dream

Clouds

Like clouds
You seemed like a soft landing
I fell for your charade

Anna Tempero

Falling

I was lost.
I'd left behind the one thing that made me, me.
He offered an opportunity,
Of course I fell.
Of course I gave him everything I had left.

What do you expect?
When the boy that became my first kiss
wanted to be my first.
When he promised I'd be his only and forever.
Was I supposed to say no?

When I couldn't tell who I was anymore
he gave me a purpose.
Of course I let myself fall.

A Whirlwind Dream

Ropes

We're just two people, tied together by two ropes.
One rope loosens but in the same moment
the other is pulled tight.
We feel a sense of freedom
only to be pulled straight back to reality.

Two ropes with different strengths
constantly picking up the other's slack.
Two people with different goals
constantly falling into the same trap.

Anna Tempero

Stabiliser

I was the stabiliser to his disorder.
In doing so his disorder spread throughout my body.
As I calmed his mind I became chaotic, apathetic.
Who were we really?
Neither of us could ever do what needed to be done.

Pain and anger flooded through; love felt like a distant memory.
In the absence of love, we found confusion and games.
Clinging to the benefits whilst struggling to block out the strain.

A Whirlwind Dream

Gaslight
(A small list of things I was told not to do)

- No emojis but the occasional smiley face
- No going out to town without me
- No flirting with other guys
- Tell me when a guy messages you
- Explain why you're messaging them
- Think about how your actions affect us

Would he do the same for me or would I be crazy?

Anna Tempero

Co-dependency

We cling to people who hurt us.
Allowing ourselves to be held by the same hands that choke us.
We feel safe in their presence.
They know our pain; they caused it.

Surrounded by people willing to help, yet we shut them out.
Why?
Was their light too bright?

That same light once shone from your own eyes.
Oh please, don't hold yourself captive.

A Whirlwind Dream

Break-up fights

We sat at opposite sides of the room.
Tears streaming down both our faces.

In my head I was begging you to leave.
I thought that if you left first maybe
I'd have the courage to leave too.

But you always stayed.
You always made it seem like this was the only way
that we were ok.
So I stayed too.

A part of me broke every time.
First at the thought of losing you, but then I became fearful that I
might never be able to leave.

Anna Tempero

"I love you"

I'm left without an option
I either tell you I love you or I leave.
But if I left where would I go?
Who am I without the title you give me.
Where can I have impact if it isn't with you.

I either tell you I love you or I hurt you further.
If I leave then we are both lost.
If I leave then you'll be alone.

I either tell you I love you or I forget my good qualities.
Because my worth is solely tied up in loving you.
Because if I don't love you then I don't love humanity.

I either tell you I love you or I love myself.
And I don't think I'm worthy of that yet.
I don't know who I am so who would I even be loving.

A Whirlwind Dream

Heart on your sleeve

For years you wore my heart on your sleeve.

Taking a part of me with you.
But not caring for its needs.

Anna Tempero

Longing

I long for the day when I no longer think of you,
it feels so out of reach.

I hope one day
I'll actually care enough to leave.

A Whirlwind Dream

Escapism

Glorifying the thought of moving away.
Again
Moving to a place where no one knows my name.

For what?
To create space?

Leaving has never solved the problems I face.

Anna Tempero

Longed

I longed for a great love.
In my head I thought it might come from you.

How could it?

I wouldn't even make room.

A Whirlwind Dream

Scared

You will always have a piece of me.
I'm scared that when I try to give that piece to someone else, it will be painful.

Anna Tempero

Desire

All of a sudden the desires of him aren't as strong.
Knowing that to love him I have to lose another.

A Whirlwind Dream

Lines

The lines are blurred.
Our feelings run deep.

How long until we fall apart again?

Anna Tempero

Cluttered

Cluttered, messy, apathetic.
All things I feel about my life.

The input far outweighing the output of my mind.

How can I find rest?

A Whirlwind Dream

Slow process

There were times when it felt like this would never end.
When I felt like I couldn't breathe.
I still feel that way sometimes, like I'll never be strong enough
to let you go.
If this wasn't the end, you'd still be here.
You left?

The ending is so much harder than the day we met.
I need strength to endure this.

Falling was easy but healing is a slow process.

Anna Tempero

Touch

For the first time in a long time
I craved your touch.

I thought I was over that at least.
Maybe I'll never be?

Will a part of me always crave my first touch?

The innocence and trust.
Where did it all go?

A Whirlwind Dream

NSFW

With one hand around my neck
and the other below my pants.
I speak harsh words over my own body.
I picture your hands and imagine your voice.
I crave your touch, still.
After all these years and all of the reasons
you've shown me not too.

Even with another man
I couldn't shake the memories of you.

When does this end?
When will I forget?

Anna Tempero

Submission

I let you use me,
I thought I needed your love.

I looked at myself as empty without it.
So I went out of my way to ensure your happiness.

I need to learn to be selfish.

A Whirlwind Dream

Charade

I have it within me to feel loved and beautiful.
To feel happy.

I shouldn't need the validation of a reply
or another person to prove this to myself.

And yet,
I still give myself away.

Constantly chasing after a charade.

Anna Tempero

Stability

I was surrounded by familiar places.
Within the same night I felt both peace and fear.

Maybe that's a representation of my mind.
Sometimes a safe place, sometimes not.

Where can I find the middle ground?
Can a place ever be stable
or does stability always have to come from within?

A Whirlwind Dream

Toxic

I say it's fine.
But it's messing with my head.

I know that it is and I keep doing it anyway.

You bring out the worst in me.
The parts I don't like to admit are mine.

We all have things we need to work on.
Suddenly mine have come to light.

Anna Tempero

Uncertainty

Confused by my feelings until it's too late.
Until the moment has passed.
Making those around me wait.
Causing unnecessary pain.
Never sure enough to actually speak out.

How can I be stronger?
Where do I find my voice?

A Whirlwind Dream

Collateral damage

I'm being selfish again.
Allowing the void I want filled to suck in another victim.
Expecting him to show me love when I can give nothing in return.

My pain is affecting the lives of innocent bystanders.
Asking them to nourish me while I just take and take.

I guess you're what they call collateral damage.
For that I am sorry.

Anna Tempero

Unfair

As much as I want to hold you
I won't let you hold on to something that you cannot have.

It's unfair of me to hold you up
and then watch as I let you fall.

I'm sorry for my lack of strength.

A Whirlwind Dream

Chains

Maybe this is just another link in the chain.
Something that needs to be broken for me to be set free.

But I don't feel free.

I just feel left and unappreciated.

Anna Tempero

Friendship

Like icy lakes in spring
our hearts are so easily cracked.

A simple unfollow sent waves through
a once thought stable place.

The concept of friendships
something I struggle to comprehend.

A Whirlwind Dream

Spiralling

It might look like spinning to you
but I feel like I'm spiralling.

Anna Tempero

Craving

You realise the things you miss
when you've been given a taste.

Still craving that attention
a single touch will send shivers down your spine.

A once strong friendship; now has grounds for temptation.

A Whirlwind Dream

Desperate

I'm gagging to be cared for.
Chasing after anything that resembles *love*.

Choking on their empty words.
Leaving myself breathless
with every lack of reply.

Anna Tempero

Compromise

It's amazing what we'll compromise to feel wanted.

A close friend
Our dignity
Peace

Apparently the feeling of being wanted
will act as a mask for our true feelings.

It distracts the usual muse of inadequacy.

A Whirlwind Dream

Lockdown

These feelings should be a sign.
Watch me go ahead and ignore them anyway.

Maybe the government will step in to save me this time.

Anna Tempero

Self-sabotage

Self-sabotage became a lot easier
when you were willing to do it alongside me.

A Whirlwind Dream

Manipulation

Manipulation feels like love.

The chase, the waiting.
It feels like home.

Once again I cling to familiarity.
I've felt like this for years.

I find peace in your affirmations and reassurance.
It's almost like you know exactly what to say
just to make me stay.

The longer I hold on to you the more I let go of myself.
Will I ever find strength?

Anna Tempero

Safety

I search for safety in the arms of men.

Even with their hands gripped around my neck
I can still find comfort.

What does it mean to find *peace* in something
that more often causes you pain.

A Whirlwind Dream

Orange

Orange was your favourite colour.
I liked that about you.

To me, the colour orange is bold.
I was drawn to the idea that you could be bold for me.
That you'd bring the healing I so desperately sought after.

Turns out orange isn't so bold after all.
It's just a watered down version of red.
You were a watered down version of him.

Of course orange looked warm and inviting when for so long
all I'd known was fiery red.

Anna Tempero

Drunken promises

'I love you'
That's what you told me
After a drunken night out.

You said 'I love you'
As if your love was strong enough to heal any pain.
As if you knew what those words really meant.

You said 'I love you'
After a drunken night out.

As if I was supposed to believe you.

A Whirlwind Dream

Suffocating

Still suffocating under the weight of his words.
They're now coming from your mouth.

I don't want to hear them.

How can I be held by you but still feel trapped in him?

I found an escape in you.
But now, once again,

I'm unable to leave.

Anna Tempero

Broken dreams

You have no idea what that felt like.
To have given him everything I had.
Just for him to go and give a piece of it to everyone else.

To then love and accept him the moment he came back.
As if there was more of myself I could give.

Maybe if I had more he could have stayed.

Even now, the pain hasn't left.
I'm still finding ways to give myself to people
who cannot hold me.

I gave what little was left of myself to somebody else, and once
again I'm left on empty.
I'm now holding a piece of two different hearts.
Sitting on a shelf along with broken dreams.
The remnants of my love, scattered between them.

I don't know how to let them go.

Do they ache for me like I do them?

A Whirlwind Dream

Autumn mornings

It's so cold
My chest hurts
I'm struggling to breathe
Struggling to forget
Anything
I can't forget anything
It's all at the forefront of my mind

Your laugh
Her eyes
That day

I want it to stop

Anna Tempero

Hate

I hate that I'm jealous.
I hate that I still care, even if it's just a little bit.

I hate that I'm not ready yet.

A Whirlwind Dream

Ache

The ache in my chest
A shallow pain that won't fade

This constant reminder

I caused pain
You are gone
I'm in pain

One million happy thoughts,
but they're all brought back to you

You.

The one that I hurt
The one I won't ever get back

Anna Tempero

Loss

You always told me that losing a best friend hurt the same
as losing a significant other.
I never understood that.

Losing him was the first worst pain I'd ever felt.
And I don't think I've ever lost a true friend.

Until now that is.
Until I lost you.

A Whirlwind Dream

High

When the high off their toxins subsides
it's your name that remains.

The thought of you that grounds me.

How can I let that go?

Anna Tempero

Sorry

I wish there was more I could say.
More that I could do for you.

I should have listened to my fears.
I should have said sorry.

I was stupid and careless,
you never deserved any of this.

I am so, so sorry.

A Whirlwind Dream

A 2020 wish

I wish I could leave this all behind and start fresh.

I wish I could reinvent myself
in a city where no one knows my past.

I wish I had the confidence to make important decisions.

I wish I had an opinion on anything without feeling like I need validation or reassurance.

I wish this year never happened.

I wish I'd been stronger.

I wish I could make up for everything I've done.

I've hurt way too many people
due to my inability to make decisions.

Anna Tempero

An ode to street fruit

Smashed pear on the pavement.
Like dreams I've thrown away to create peace.
A reminder of pain and pressure.

Juice splatters imitate the chaos that always seems to
follow my decisions.

Fresh fruit scattered along the roadside.
Symbolising hope for another day.
I watch as they lie blissfully unaware of their fate.

A Whirlwind Dream

Intrusive thoughts

Trying to remind myself what I'm worth,
but struggling to believe it.

How can I speak light into my own world
when I don't think that I deserve it.

Anna Tempero

Potential

I can't heal my heart while being pursued by you.

I cannot reach my full potential
while continually pining for yours.

A Whirlwind Dream

Tug of war

I'm in a tug of war.
It's a fight between the person I am now
and the person I want to become.

It's an uneven fight.
A constant battle.

The pull of my current life outweighs that of the future.

I begin to move forward
but I'm jolted back by fear and doubt.

I have to keep fighting.

Anna Tempero

Identity

I'm surrounded by thoughts and feelings of the world.
Trapped by multiple personalities.
Too timid to portray mine.
Stuck being the person I've always been to appease the constraints
I built myself.

My identity moulds to fit the atmosphere of a room.
I'm constantly a different person.
Which parts of 'me' should stay?

A Whirlwind Dream

Timing

Our timing was always off and you are still proving that.

Anna Tempero

Covid-19

I'm just so lucky that I am where I am.
And I often complain, I do, but when I feel down I don't understand it. And I was never given the tools to express it. And so, when I'm down I do everything I can to suppress it or hide it or act as though everything is fine.
But we all know that fine is not fine, and every time I do this to myself I get angrier. Why can I not just admit that I'm sad or scared or lonely? And I look to all of my friends; they all speak so freely. And I get jealous. I end up resenting the people who care for me, all because I don't have the strength to be honest. But if I'm honest, then I'll tell them that I am sad and scared and lonely but know that I don't deserve to be. And I'll explain to them all of the reasons why my feelings are invalid, and I'll just change the subject so we can talk about them.
Why can I not just let my friends be my friends and my feelings be my feelings. This all seems so trivial, and -even while writing- I'm judging myself again for trying to make my situation sound worse than it is, but it's just that; my situation. Covid-19 makes me feel trapped. It's like I'm walking towards my future, but with every step I take another piece of the wall caves in around me. In its absence is a deep abyss of darkness. It feels as though with every turn I take my chest will become tighter, and all of a sudden there won't be enough air to breathe.

A Whirlwind Dream

Run

I want to run to you.
Even now, even still.

Anna Tempero

Defence

How are you still a defence mechanism for me?
How am I still struggling to let go?

I want to cut ties
but I'm still going out of my way to nurture them.

How do I break free?

A Whirlwind Dream

Safe

I felt safe with him.

Not because he made me feel that way.
But because he made everything else around me feel unsafe.

Anna Tempero

PPE

You tore me down, and I saw it as protection.
Hence why I still search for safety in your presence.

A Whirlwind Dream

Box

You shut me in, and I would lock the door.
Being controlled was easier than taking
a hold of my own true feelings.

Anna Tempero

Confusion

Familiarity/safety
Two words often confused as one.

Sometimes they'll go hand in hand.

But not with them
Not with you

I cling to our familiarity, but you are not my safe place.

A Whirlwind Dream

How?

How can I exert enough strength for my friends to find comfort and confidence in their own bodies?
When I myself have days where I look at the number on the scales and wish that it was less.
How can I assure my friends that their health will improve?
When I worry that my own body won't be able to do the
one thing I want most.

How can I have enough strength to be strong enough for the people who need me?
When often I'm not even strong enough for myself.

Can somebody please tell me how?

Anna Tempero

Stuck

Stuck between two realities.
There's the truth and the ideas I come up with in my head.
I constantly get hurt.
People can't live up to the expectations I don't express.

The lines aren't connected.
Everything is a blur.
I follow one line just to be confronted with a dead end.
But in my mind I create a bridge.

The picture I paint is often a far cry from reality.

Can the cloudiness explain my actions?
Or am I using my 'chaotic' mind as an excuse?

A Whirlwind Dream

Trapped

Trapped by the obligation of friendships.
By my past selves.
Trapped in a vortex of my own mind.

Even when I attempt to escape I never find freedom.
I break one wall down just to be faced with another
twice as high.

Sometimes I feel like I'll never live in a space
that feels completely free.

Anna Tempero

Grounding

When I'm in the world the world is also in me.

Spinning
    Turning
        Evolving

I have no way of controlling it.
Their thoughts become my thoughts.
My temptations become my desires
and the world in me enhances that.

I search for a grounding,
I have to claw myself back.
Before I am theirs and no longer mine.
Before I forget where I end and they begin.

A Whirlwind Dream

Birds

Have you ever been jealous of birds?
Of their freedom.

A bird doesn't feel empty with every lack of reply.
They aren't weighed down by the constraints of society.
Their lives are not measured by their 'success'.

Oh to be a bird.
To be able to spread my wings.

Anna Tempero

OCD

I read the screen 20 times over.
My palms begin to sweat.
It's still not enough to satisfy.

I refresh the page, again and again.
It has to feel right this time.

My mind is a vortex.
I don't know when to stop.

The repetitions get worse as the day progresses.
The paranoia kicks in,
can anyone see this?

Do they watch as I take in deep breaths again?
Do they notice the pause as I stare at a page and wait for my mind to comprehend?

A Whirlwind Dream

Social media

I get so caught up on these messages as though one reply equates to the sum of my greatness.

My body hangs by a thread
as I refresh the screen once more.

Stomach in angst
Head in the clouds
Waiting on the moment I can breathe again.

Anna Tempero

Nightmares

I dream about it still.

Him and her
Me and them
The angst and misery

Even whilst asleep I can still feel my body's tension.
I wake up relieved but with a tinge of sadness.
I'm not over it yet,
I haven't fully healed.
The reminders are still too real.

It's during these nights that my sins become ten fold
when I'm reminded of my past self without
acknowledging the one I'm becoming.

I wonder if they too dream about me.
Are their thoughts intruded by this never ending pain?

A Whirlwind Dream

Lies

If I believed the lies they told just to make me stay.
How can I expect to accept honest words of love?

Anna Tempero

Intimacy

I feel heavy in the arms of men.
My chest tightens.
My heart beats faster.
I have to concentrate on comfort.
Block out any strain.

Touch being their main love language, yet
I have no way to reciprocate.
For their touch brings more pain than good.

I give in to any temptation but only in an attempt to please.
In an attempt to find happiness in the arms of different men.
But ending up right back in his.
Right back under him.

It feels as though there is no escape.
No arms that could ease my restraint.

A Whirlwind Dream

Pleasure

You don't want me.
You want the idea of me.

What more can my hands give you than a soulless connection.
Hearing your plea does not uplift me.
It's just another reminder.

My body is merely a vessel for pleasure.
Not a being to be cared for.

Anna Tempero

Body count

Their body on top of mine never loses weight.
The faces and names may change
but the feeling remains the same.

Trapped
        Controlled
                Hopeless

How can one man ruin the path for every man ahead?

A Whirlwind Dream

Coercion

I was hesitant, he kept persisting.
I pulled back, he kept pushing.

This time ended in happiness for us both.
This time I willingly put myself under his spell.

I feel guilty for the words I've previously used.
Because this time I wanted it.
This time I allowed it.

Bad behaviour is one thing but allowing it is another.
Enjoying it is something I'm still trying to comprehend.

Where is the line between coercion and consent?

Anna Tempero

Indirect

Maybe I was too indirect.
Or did I speak in a way that didn't allow him to dissect?

What I was saying or how I was feeling.
Who I am or what I need.

A Whirlwind Dream

Heartbreaker

Being a heartbreaker was all well and good when I was a kid.
There were no repercussions.
No past traumas.

I could say no without feeling the weight of the world
for weeks afterwards.

These days saying no feels like less of an option.

Anna Tempero

Misunderstood

He left feeling like a poetry prompt.
Unsure of his meaning, questioning his worth.
I trampled on his heart with a few quick stomps.

The insecurities never let our qualities speak.
Too many 'I don't knows'
and yet not enough conversation.
Too many pushes but not enough pulling.

Our wires constantly finding themselves crossed.
Never did I expect him to be the one leaving lost.

A Whirlwind Dream

Blurred lines

I thought we were on the same page.
I guess the ink looks different through each set of eyes.

Anna Tempero

Unnecessary ending

The flowers were left to wilt,
now you're forced to avoid my name.

It wasn't supposed to end like this.

A Whirlwind Dream

Acetone

The acetone in my system
Led me to you
Led me to us
Led me to her
Led me to them

My mind is chaos
Swirling
Churning
Tumbling
It won't stop

I don't understand
I don't understand
This doesn't make sense

Why are you still here
Why do I still care
Why
Why am I so frustrated just by the thought of her

I do not understand
It's too much
My thoughts are too much

How do I stop
How does it end
Will this ever end

It's gotten to that point again
Again
Already
We're back to that space of angst

Anna Tempero

I don't understand
I was doing so well
How am I back here
How are you here
Again
Always you

Why not him
He didn't say happy birthday
Why does that thought not bother me

It doesn't make sense
I don't make sense

The acetone in my system led me to you
You
Why is it always you
Will it ever be me

Maybe it was me
Can you tell me where I went wrong
Did I go wrong

I don't understand
I don't understand

Repetitions
Affirmations
Self-despair

My head is swirling
Why are you here
The acetone in my system led me to us
The thought of your Mum

A Whirlwind Dream

The many what ifs
Would you call me if Saber died
Why do I still think like this
Why do I still care

The acetone in my system led me to me
And I didn't like what I saw
When will I like what I see
I thought that I was free

But now I'm here
The acetone in my system led me here
Here to you
Here to them
Here to God

But I can't be everywhere
And I can't be here.

DREAMS

A Whirlwind Dream

Free

Do I feel free because I've stopped trying.
Do I feel as though a weight has been lifted simply because
I've given up?

Is this self-destruction?

Anna Tempero

Survivors guilt

How can I heal the pain that was never mine to begin with?
How do I overcome sorrow
that I myself cannot even comprehend?

How can I be so thankful and free
while the world around me crumbles?

A Whirlwind Dream

Craving

Still craving the part of you I see in every guy I meet.

Anna Tempero

Control

She watches as the waves go back and forth.
It reminds her of him,
the way he always comes and goes.
Giving her a taste and then swiftly pulling back.

She wishes she was the moon.
Then she'd have control over his motions.

A Whirlwind Dream

Wellington

I miss the Wellington flat.
The infinite feeling of freedom.

I miss the way we could be together.
The absence of judgment.

It was just you and me.
And that was all that it had to be.

Anna Tempero

Love

I don't want to let you go.

I just want to give you and everyone else
the love they deserve.

A Whirlwind Dream

Savour

Is there space in my heart
that holds room for all the people I've loved?
Is there a way of keeping them with me?
Of picking them up
and placing them down along the way.
I am not myself without the pieces of their love embedded in my
thoughts and mannerisms.
The person I am was built on our interactions.

Can I remember them without hindering my future.
Can our stories be celebrated whilst dealing with the pain.

Anna Tempero

Fluctuation

I'm sick of fluctuation.
Sick of wavering.
For years I've been stuck in a state of turbulence.

I want to be still.

I want pride to be a constant expression for me.
I want to be confident in who I am
and what I've achieved.

I want to be strong.
I want to be loved.

A Whirlwind Dream

Loyalties

Where do my loyalties lie?
To whom should I give my attention?
Which parts of me deserve to stay
and who am I without these people.

I have this *crisis* at least once a week.

Who can I be myself around and how do I define that?
By longevity or aura.
Because they've always been
or because of who they are?
Do I hold on or choose to let go?

My heart hasn't yet grasped the concept of love's format.

Anna Tempero

Holding on

I let new memories overshadow the past.
Continuing to blur my concept of who you are.
I cling to any remains of happiness we still hold.

If I force myself to see the truth
then I have no choice but to let you go.

A Whirlwind Dream

High hopes

My memory of you is blurred.
Like a foggy morning gazing up at the tip of a mountain.
I don't see the treacherous climb
just an idea of the views from the top.
Like the little orange flowers at school,
standing beautifully proud but poisonous to touch.

My mind has been trained to see only the good in you.
In us.

Anna Tempero

An honest love

You are good
And yet here I am
Still craving the one who hurt me

Looking at my body as if it were something he'd be proud of.
Something he'd desire.

Why is it that the broken cling to the ones who hurt them?
Why is it that your heart,
so pure and genuine, isn't enough to pull me from my past?

I pray that I won't cause you pain.
That I won't let the hurt that I know
be the sword in your chest.

A Whirlwind Dream

Mirror

There are still moments
when I'll look in the mirror and see you.
Your physical hands may not be there anymore
but I can feel where they've been.
I can trace the lines.

I am getting better.
Often I'll admire my own body without looking through the lens
of your eyes.

It's a journey, I suppose.
Healing the parts of me that were ripped open in the aftermath of
our 'love'.

Anna Tempero

Words

This morning I woke to the words 'you are beautiful'.
Dozens of times throughout the day I spoke these words
over my own body.
Reminding myself of my strength and worth.

I then caught myself imagining the words
coming from your mouth instead.

Does this still equate to self-love?

If I rewrite the way you treated me,
can I find healing in my own words?

A Whirlwind Dream

Body image

We look in the mirror
our minds scream at us to look away.
We take a photo and automatically call ourselves names.

We're searching through the standards of others
wishing we were the same.

But we are love.
We are hearts that have overcome.
Bodies with so much life to live.

If only we could see through each other's eyes.

Anna Tempero

Touch

He held me.
As he did, all of my broken pieces felt like they were being carefully put back together.
So used to them being torn apart, my mind kept pulling me back to the pain I was once dealt.
His gentle kisses brought me to peace.

As he caressed my arms it felt like every touch was healing another piece of my broken past.
It was almost as if the more I was touched by him the less I was touched by you.

My body, held by his.
Felt like home.

A Whirlwind Dream

Clean slate

You gave me a clean slate.
A fresh start after so much pain.

The way you honoured my value
has realigned my entire world view.

Anna Tempero

Park boy with the nice smile

To the boy in the park,
our interaction was short but sweet.

One look at you reminded me of who I am,
the person before my first heart break,
the girl behind the mask.

Thank you
To the boy in the park

A Whirlwind Dream

The news

There's no denying my thoughts weren't altered.
It came as a shock but it wasn't painful.
There was more of you in my head than in reality.

I hope she brings the happiness you deserved all along.

Your friendship impacted me in a way I will never forget.
For that I am thankful.

Anna Tempero

Thank you

I could say that I hate you.
But tonight I wouldn't mean it.

Tonight I want to thank you.
Thank you for proving to me that in time I will find love
in another set of arms.
For allowing me space to find beauty within myself again.

Thank you for holding me up.
Even when that meant letting me go.

A Whirlwind Dream

Orion's Belt

My Orion's Belt.
I look for you in the night sky.
You held me together when life became loose.
Your grip tightened my abilities.

As soon as you let go, I fell.
But in falling I learnt how to fly.

My brightness was only ever dimmed.
You allowed me space to rediscover my light.

Anna Tempero

Side step

I looked at these men as though they were a vessel.
Transport to bring me closer to my true self.

I thought that as they held me
the weight of his arms would slowly fade.

I am fooled for only a moment.
In the end they were just another step to one side.

No less painful, no more loving.

A Whirlwind Dream

Not enough

For a while I regretted not taking advantage of the risky
opportunities in my past.
I came to understand that the part of me holding on to these ideals
is the same part of me that won't let him go.

If I'd said yes more often.
If I'd been *happier*.

Maybe things would have worked out.
Maybe he wouldn't have left.

Anna Tempero

Future me checklist

Oh to live in a space that isn't weighed down.
To be loved without constraint.

I wish to live a life of freedom.
To love without causing pain.

The way he loved kept me bound.
The way I loved wore me down.

Oh to have an opinion within a crowd.
To make friends and keep them around.

I wish to be myself within any space.
To have confidence throughout the whole race.

A Whirlwind Dream

Walls

It's like I'm surrounded by walls.
I can't tell which ones keep me safe anymore.

Do I feel trapped by your walls that can simply be broken?
Are my insecurities the glue holding them together?

Was the comfort I found in him just the space he allowed
to ensure I stayed?

Maybe your walls are meant to change me.

Anna Tempero

You.

You make me feel like I deserve more.
Like I can be whoever I want to be.
With you I want to be known.
You remind me of the light in my life.
Remind me to consistently look toward the future.
All I've ever known can be found in you.

You can't be the one to save me.
But, thank you.

But You.

You've been there from the start.
You know more of me than anyone ever has.
You teach me to be free and spontaneous.
Teach me that good things can come from a cruel place.
With you I'm constantly forced out of my comfort zone.
Constantly learning about myself and others.
All I've ever known is challenged by you.

You can't be the one to save me.
But, thank you.

A Whirlwind Dream

Beauty

I search for beauty amongst pain.

-The warmth of the sun against my face.
-The authenticity in a conversation with a stranger.
-The safety of a familiar place.

Such little gifts we often forget to embrace.

I strive to find the light in my darkness.

-The hope for a brighter day.
-The space created for growth.
-The fight to find another way.

I push forward towards my future.

I will not wait to be saved.
My own mind will be my saviour.

Anna Tempero

Sun

Sometimes I feel like the Sun; I'm bold and beautiful,
and I aim to give light to the world.
I bring warmth, but often I get stuck in the clouds, and all of a sudden my warmth can't be felt and I can't see the impact I have on anybody -let alone myself- and I don't know how to remind myself that the clouds will always leave.
How do I remind myself that my warmth will be felt once again. The clouds are showing my beauty; they show my work and my fight. I'm just tired of being the sun and feeling as though I have to light everyone else up when I'm feeling so dark within myself, and everything feels as though it's on fire.

But that fire is the light; that fire is what makes me who I am, it's what brings hope and passion.

The fire, the darkness, the clouds;
they're all necessary aspects of who I am.

A Whirlwind Dream

Dream

I dream of a day
when I no longer search for flowers in other people.

When instead I let the garden inside of me
flourish for all to see.

Anna Tempero

Hope

Surrounded by growth and beauty,
parts of me have fallen but I still have hope.
I dreamt of a mountain range
with waterfalls at every angle.

I was in awe.

Overwhelmed by an incredible sense of peace.
For if God can create such beauty in the mountains
imagine what he can create in me.

A Whirlwind Dream

World view

It's amazing how your view of the world changes
when you're in love.
Whether that be love for yourself or love for another.

When I began to find love within myself again
the way I interacted with the world transformed.
I began to find beauty in the simplest of interactions.

The sun became my muse.
Suddenly the moon brought me to tears
and laughter became music to my ears.

Anna Tempero

My saviour

I see you in the stars at night.
I find you in the clouds that light up the sky.
I notice you as I watch families play in the park.

Lord, you are everywhere and yet you are here.
Meeting me, right where I need you.
Meeting me even when I think you're not near.

Every time I run, it's you who chases me.
When I fall it's you who catches me.
I have never reached for you and not
had you pull me back to safety.

How lucky am I.

A Whirlwind Dream

Forgiving myself

I think it's beautiful that you still see him as a bright light.
That you choose to remember the good times
and forget the bad.
Maybe you should have forced these boundaries
a long time ago, and maybe you let him away
with more than you can comprehend.

But look how far you've come.

Anna Tempero

Creation

Although starry nights are now laced with you, and the sun cannot set without thoughts of her.

I will always find beauty in creation.

A Whirlwind Dream

The Sun

She beamed at me as she sat nestled
between two buildings.
Her warmth fills me
from the moment her rays make contact with my face.
I smile, she always finds a way to touch me.
I'm in awe of her talent.
I watch as she illuminates every surface in view.
The bright yellow leaves in Autumn.
The reddened hills at dusk.
Light pink clouds caressing her sky.
I'm jealous of birds for they get closer to her
than I'll ever be.

My first real muse.
I will forever be in search of you.

Anna Tempero

Quarantine

Oh quarantine.
You allowed me space to find rest.
My previous loves trapped me in a way that caused distress.
You lovingly created boundaries that freed me.
Initially I was fearful,
in the past I'd been held back by constraints.
But your rules, they kept me safe.
You caused my world to slow down just enough so that I could
regain balance.
Before we met I was stumbling and tired.
You brought me peace.
In a time when chaos penetrated the earth,
your stronghold kept me sane.
You reminded me of the beauty of stillness.
The blessing of nature.
You reignited a passion in my soul.
I sat and watched as families played.
Couples were reaffirming their love for one another.
Beauty is so easily found when life is stripped back.
I can't thank you enough.
May we meet again in different light.

Oh quarantine
I will never forget you.

A Whirlwind Dream

Riptide

We are the sea.
You are a riptide.
I am caught in the power you possess.

But I become stronger with each attempt.
Soon I'll be able to swim against the current.
Soon your weight will no longer pull me down.

I will use your force to create momentum.

Anna Tempero

Growth

Your happiness no longer represents my demise.
I too am living a free and authentic life.

We both have a chance now.
I just have to remember my growth.

A Whirlwind Dream

Euphoria

You're here and you are breathing.
You're happy and you're allowed to be.
Those feelings that come to light on a Friday night.
They are still true.
Substances may have enhanced the way you felt
but that feeling is attainable.

It all comes from your own mind.
You have to find healthy ways to cultivate that.
Like sunrise missions or the sound of waves.
Poetry in a cafe or music in your ears.
Do more of the things that bring happiness and those feelings will naturally resurface.

You are not broken.
You're pieces that have been shattered.
You are slowly coming back together.

Allow yourself the same grace you so easily give away.

Anna Tempero

Emulate

My character emulates the moon.
I am ever changing.
I'm pulled by the gravity of the world.

I reflect the light of the *sun*.

My identity shifts in correlation with my journey.
And I only show my full self every so often,
cautious of being too bold.

A Whirlwind Dream

Voice

I'm beginning to find my voice.
It is both terrifying and exciting.

My desire for peace and harmony often restricts it.

But I'm learning that my opinion has value.
Even when it differs from those around me.

Anna Tempero

Power

When I began to say no
I started to realise the power I held all along.

I vow to never lose sight of that again.

A Whirlwind Dream

Cacophony

My life in cacophony;

Disruptive
    Dishonest
        Despaired

Oh to live a life in symphony;

Uniting
    Uplifting
        Empowering

My life caught up in noise.
With unity it could become a masterpiece.

Anna Tempero

Pieces

When my pieces began falling into place
instead of just falling.

That's when I knew life was changing for the better.

A Whirlwind Dream

Self-talk

The lies I tell myself
have become ever prominent since I began dismissing them.
When I stepped out of my comfort zone
the lies became louder and louder
so as though I wouldn't forget them as I left.

Sadly for my lies
the truths I now cling to have a stronger voice.

OUR REALITY

OUR REALITY

A Whirlwind Dream

For the best

This is for the best.
You're going to be ok.

They will move on if you let them.
You have to be strong for the both of you.

You are loved and worthy of so much more.

They have friends and family who will care for them.
It is not your job to bring them hope.

(Repeat until you're ok again.)

Anna Tempero

Sunrise

The sun will always rise.
Teach yourself to find the horizon again.

Position yourself to look for the light.
You are strong enough to emerge from the darkness.

A Whirlwind Dream

Infliction

It is almost never about you.
Their bad behaviour more often than not stems from their own insecurities as opposed to your inadequacy.

Anna Tempero

Deflecting

The unnecessary pain you're afflicting
should be what you're most afraid of.
Don't let the actions of past lovers turn you
into someone you are not.

Inflicting pain on others will only hurt you further.

Allow yourself space to heal.
Be open and honest.

You can grow from this.

A Whirlwind Dream

Truth telling

We can't fix our problems whilst lying to ourselves.
We cannot heal from the actions of others if we're
fooling ourselves about who they are and how they treated us.

Anna Tempero

Letting go

I've found the hardest part of letting go
is acknowledging pain.
It's throwing away the ideals we keep in our minds.
It means we have to see things for how they are
instead of how we want them to be.
Acknowledging that we too may have caused pain.

That's the hardest part of letting go.
But holding on is just as painful.
Holding on keeps you stagnant.

Have courage to step forward.
Make room for freedom.

A Whirlwind Dream

Rain

For the rain has come before, and it left.
It can happen again.
Let it pass through you.
Use the moisture for growth on the other side.

Acknowledge its presence without letting yourself drown.

Anna Tempero

5 reasons to say no

1. If you are going out of your way and giving too much of yourself for the happiness of somebody else.

2. If you feel as though a particular relationship gives you an upper hand over your closest friends.

3. If a part of you is doing it to 'get over' someone else.

4. When you are putting friendships and collateral relationships at risk. You still need those people.

5. If you think this person is an answer to your problems. They may make you feel good, but can they make you happy? Being genuinely happy and feeling good are not the same thing.

A Whirlwind Dream

Ideal

They are not the person you see in them.
Remember that.

Don't fall for the person you have in mind.

Sacrifice

The moment caring for someone else starts to dishonour your own
character or identity is the moment it becomes
an unhealthy attachment.

If caring for someone begins to degrade you *that is not love*.
Love requires sacrifice, but it shouldn't directly cause you pain.

A Whirlwind Dream

Affirmations

You're a lot stronger than you often portray yourself as being.
You are worthy of the love you desire.
You are capable of being a genuine friend.
Even when life is turbulent you are growing.
You still have time.
It's ok to explore things that bring you happiness.
It's ok to change.
You don't always have to be the person you used to be.
You don't have to change to fit in with the right people.
Time alone to work on yourself is necessary.
Saying no is ok.
It's ok to admit when you have been treated badly.
It's ok to have positive memories
of people who have hurt you.
You don't have to live within
the constraints of your pain.
But don't downplay your feelings.
Everyone feels pain differently, and your pain is valid.

(A list of things to remind yourself.)

Anna Tempero

Motivation

There are things we have to go through that aren't
a now or never situation. We can't try our best for one day and
expect things to change. Sometimes it has to be a
"now and then and then and then" situation.

You have to push through, pace yourself.
You can't give up after the first hurdle.
You have to trust and apply yourself over and over again.

You get to a point when you feel like you can't keep going, and
that's when you have to push harder and faster.
It has to keep happening.

It's easy to compare and judge, but you need to focus on your end
goal; the goals of others are unattainable.
When you're trying something for the first time, you cannot expect
yourself to perform at your best.

Your best takes practice and perseverance.
Think of a time where you've accomplished a goal; did it happen
all at once or did you have work for it again and again?
Give your thoughts and your health the same opportunities you
would for your chosen sport or passion.

Keep trying for better times.
Allow yourself to feel.
Align yourself with people who can hold you steadfast.

A Whirlwind Dream

The healing process

You will weave in and out of your ability to change.
This is inevitable.
The moment you decide to heal isn't the moment you forget.

Memories will resurface, and
to overcome a feeling we have to feel it to its extent.
But don't give up.
Rest when you need to and pick up again from where you left off.

Recognise that the re-feeling isn't the initial blow.
You are safe now; find spaces where you can explore that deep
feeling long enough to understand it.

Surround yourself with people who will hold you up so that you're
in a space where you can be vulnerable.

Anna Tempero

Healing

It's ok if there is still more grieving to be done.
It's ok if the tightness in your chest
returns from time to time.
The hurt was so engrained in your routine, it's understandable that
happiness feels out of place.
Give yourself time.
Listen to these feelings,
let them push you towards more.
Remind yourself of the freedom you've felt before.
This isn't a setback.
It doesn't mean you're not ready.
It just means there is still healing to be done.
That's ok.
Learn to let people in.
Have trust that the right person will know exactly how to hold the
pieces that are still being put back together.

(For days when the pain returns and you feel like you'll never be able to move on.)

A Whirlwind Dream

Effort

Treat each step as if it is crucial.
Focus on doing things that are right for you.
Teach yourself to make healthy and informed decisions.
Create space to realise what that means for you.
Learn to say no to things that no longer serve you.
Find a fresh sense of freedom and healing.

You will regain happiness.

As you continue to reflect you will continue to heal.

3 tips towards healing.

1. Once you normalise an action you give away consent for someone to treat you in that way. Understand your boundaries and hold on to them.

2. You must listen to your bad memories in order to overcome them. Solely remembering the good times will only prolong your suffering.

3. Speaking your truth is not an insult. You shouldn't feel guilty for expressing how someone's actions have affected you.

A Whirlwind Dream

Rising sun

You are the rising sun.
On its way up after a fall.
Slowly building from the rubble of a broken life.

The rising sun.
A constant reminder of a new day.
A reminder that no matter where you've been,
you can always start again.

The rising sun.
Full of colour and light.
Just like your ever-evolving self.

Anna Tempero

Rise

I can promise you,
that when you begin to heal and give yourself credit
for all the things you've been through,

You will start to feel beautiful again.

A Whirlwind Dream

Learning

Above all else you are still learning.
Through learning comes growth.

You don't have to be at your end goal to acknowledge progress.

I know you will be ok in the end, and when the end comes you will gracefully accept the new beginnings.

Anna Tempero

Remember

This doesn't have to be a setback.
Remember how much you've grown.
You are so much stronger than you were before.

A Whirlwind Dream

Focus

Focus on how you feel.
Knowing how someone else is feeling
will only change the way you're feeling.
How someone feels doesn't change the part you played in making
them feel that way.
Make decisions based off how you feel
and what you want.

No matter how hard you try
changing the feelings of others is an unattainable goal.

(For when you feel yourself making decisions to ease the pain of someone else whilst inflicting pain on yourself in the process.)

Anna Tempero

Feel

Please can you just let yourself feel.
You don't always have to compare
or try to understand others.
If you're feeling bad one day and then good the next
that's ok, you're lucky.
Take that blessing and run with it.

It's your life and your feelings.
No matter how hard you try
you have no control over the feelings of others.

Nurture your own mind, trust your own feelings.

A Whirlwind Dream

Grace

I think one of the most important aspects of healing is actually
showing yourself grace.
It means that when you mess up
you aren't so hard on yourself.
Of course you have to recognise patterns, and you need to want to
do better, but don't beat yourself up.
Do your best to resist temptation, but if it becomes too much and
you give in this time; don't get discouraged.
Don't automatically write yourself off.
Just pick yourself up again.
Remind yourself of the growth and freedom you've found, and
keep putting in the effort to maintain and strengthen that.
Some days or weeks will be harder than others
but *stay the course*.

Keep pushing for more, always.

Anna Tempero

Afraid

You're so afraid of losing the people close to you
and so okay with losing yourself in the process.
If you can't value yourself, you won't genuinely value others.

Use that same motivation to fight for yourself.
Use that dead-weight positivity to uplift your own passions.

(For days when you're pursuing the happiness of others in place of exploring and uplifting your own.)

A Whirlwind Dream

Sure

Make sure to know who you are, and what you want,
before giving yourself to someone else.

Any uncertainty will hurt you.

Anna Tempero

Desires

Let your desires be fluid.
Allow them to travel with you
as the people you love come and go.
Find joy in these things with each person you define special,
and learn to create ways to keep that passion alive
as each person may pass.

Your desires don't always have to be attached to a person or place.
It's ok to continually take them with you.

A Whirlwind Dream

Travel

There is so much more to the world than a small town
filled with people who have hurt you.

Go out and explore it.

Anna Tempero

Silver platter

You look at the bare minimum
as if it's been served to you on a silver platter.
Start to imagine how it might feel
to be truly loved and cared for.

You cling to the smallest crevasses.
Learn to wait for the stepping stones.

A Whirlwind Dream

Phantom pains

Chains when they are too tight create wounds.
They break the skin.
Your pain does not mean the chains are still bound.
It means your hurt runs deeper than the surface.
You still have wounds to heal.
Scars that aren't fully covered yet.

You are no longer trapped.

Anna Tempero

Live

When you begin to live your life without requiring validation, there you will find freedom.

Eat your dinner without sharing it with the world.
Watch that movie without telling your friends you cried.
Enjoy new music before sharing it with someone else.

Live in a way that brings you happiness, and don't wait on someone else's response to confirm that.

> *You smiled*
>   *You laughed*
>   *You danced*

Take joy in those moments.
You don't always have to let others in.
People can't always reciprocate your joy.

Just live my darling, be free.

(For days when the opinions or reactions of others cause you to become disheartened.)

A Whirlwind Dream

Its ok

It's ok to find happiness and peace following pain.
It's ok to grow from your mistakes.

Learning won't take away the pain.
But growth creates room for forgiveness.

It's ok for you to have a fresh start.
It's ok to keep trying.

Anna Tempero

Wildflowers

Like wildflowers, we bloom and we die.
We rise and we fall.
As seasons pass, parts of us are broken.
But eventually we're made whole again.
The beauty is always regained.

Let the falling leaves remind you to always
find rest in times of fullness.

A Whirlwind Dream

Community

Don't count yourself out,
even when you think you deserve to be.
You deserve so much more than you allow yourself.

Don't isolate yourself.
Even when you can't, others will see your worth.
Let them remind you of who you could be.

Anna Tempero

Seaside

She sat seaside.
Listening to the sounds of waves breaking in the distance.
The laughter between friends and family.
Her hair flows softly in the wind.

As she sits, with a book in her hand and the sun on her neck.
She feels as close to her authentic self as she has in years.

Comfortable.
In her body, mind and self.

She knew she was finally beginning to break free of her shells.

She is me.
She can be you too.

A Whirlwind Dream

A great love

Don't let the hints of disappointment deter you.
Let these feelings be motivation for what's to come.

You deserve this, you will find this.

(For days when another one of your friends finds love.)

Anna Tempero

Worthy

The tightness in your chest does not dismiss your growth.
It doesn't change your worth or your freedom.
That pain will be felt from time to time, but it shouldn't stop you
from pursuing a chance at love.
Push into opportunities placed in front of you.
Embrace change and happiness.
You deserve this and so much more.
Don't belittle yourself in fear of what's been.
You are so much stronger than you were back then.
Have faith in yourself but also the world.
Not everyone is out to harm you.

(For when you're starting to get back out there.)

A Whirlwind Dream

For days when you feel like the moon.

The moon is only ever visible when it reflects light from the sun.
You must constantly search for the sun.
Look for people and things that illuminate you.
Things that make you happy or highlight who you are.
Explore places that inspire you.
Spend time with people who only want to see you shine.
The darkness, although terrifying and all-consuming, is a beautiful opportunity for you to shine brighter.
To me, a moon or a star that is shining brightly amongst darkness
can be more beautiful than the sun
that has only ever known light.
The moon is constantly changing shape.
And maybe you do too.
Or maybe you just change your moods
depending on who you're with.
This isn't a sign of weakness.
It shows that life isn't linear.
It shows the ups and downs that come with a life of pursuing light.
It's a reminder that sometimes
only giving part of yourself away is healthy.
Sometimes it's safer to show only a part of who you are.
The moon changes shape, but in the end
it always comes back to a whole.
You will too, even on days when you feel like a new moon and
nothing around you is light.

Anna Tempero

2017

2017 me never thought she would feel this free.

And yet here I am, dancing in my living room again.
Celebrating the small victories and looking forward
to all that's still to come.

2017 me was scared, trapped and in pain.
But here I am.
Baring the scars and learning how to be patient in my mistakes.

2017 me didn't know who she was.
But I can look back now and see exactly
how far I've come.

Give yourself time.
You will always heal.
You will always find yourself.

Write a letter to yourself.
Reflect on the nightmares; make sense of your reality;
dare to dream!

_____

_____

_____

_____

_____

_____

_____

_____

_____

_____

_____

_____

_____

_____

_____

About the author

Photo by Courtney Jane Smith - @janecourtney1996

Anna Tempero is a self-published writer who, much like everyone else, uses writing as a way to calm her mind.
It was Anna's best kept secret to one day publish a poetry book; it's now here for the world to see.
As Anna grew up, she frequently struggled to express her feelings, especially to those she cared about most.
This compilation of work gives the reader a peak into her ever-evolving mind. Anna is currently pursuing a Bachelor's degree in Counselling and is actively trying to understand her own mind and those of the world around her.

www.ingramcontent.com/pod-product-compliance
Lightning Source LLC
Chambersburg PA
CBHW011150290426
44109CB00025B/2558